RETAILED'S RETAIL STORE OPENING & CLOSING PROCEDURES

A workbook for opening and closing a store.

Laura De La Cruz

Copyright © 2016 by High Chaparral Publishing. All rights reserved worldwide.

No part of this publication may be replicated, redistributed, or given away in any form without the prior written consent of the author/publisher or the terms relayed to you herein.

High Chaparral Publishing

75 County Road A074

Chaparral, NM 88081

www.highchaparralpublishing.com

HOW TO USE THIS JOURNAL/WORKBOOK

Opening and closing a store is a process that can be made easier if you have a checklist. Use this workbook so your employees never forget what needs to be done when opening or closing your store!

Opening Checklist

Date _____

- ☐ Arrive 15-30 minutes prior to opening
- ☐ Perform a visual check, if concerned call 911
- ☐ Never open the store alone, always have at least one other coworker present
- ☐ Unlock door, turn off alarm, relock door
- ☐ Perform another visual check inside
- ☐ Turn on lights
- ☐ Open safe, remove cash register tills
- ☐ Count money (in office)
- ☐ Turn on computers
- ☐ Turn on air or heat
- ☐ Start daily task list
- ☐ Prepare lunch and break schedules
- ☐ Activate displays, turn on televisions/radios
- ☐ Place/take down display signs as needed
- ☐ Check e-mail and respond if necessary
- ☐ _____
- ☐ _____

Closing Checklist

Date _____

- ☐ After all customers have left, lock door(s)
- ☐ Bring any product from outside into the store
- ☐ Extinguish exterior and front lights
- ☐ Place "closed" sign
- ☐ Close out registers
- ☐ Clean and restock restrooms
- ☐ Return all non-defective merchandise to shelves
- ☐ Move defective merchandise to back room
- ☐ Dust and mop, empty trash
- ☐ Count registers and balance
- ☐ Settle all credit card machines
- ☐ Generate detailed batch listing
- ☐ Transmit batch
- ☐ Place all tills in safe and lock
- ☐ Turn off all electronic equipment
- ☐ Set the alarm, exit and lock doors
- ☐ _____
- ☐ _____

Opening Checklist

Date _____

- ❑ Arrive 15-30 minutes prior to opening
- ❑ Perform a visual check, if concerned call 911
- ❑ Never open the store alone, always have at least one other coworker present
- ❑ Unlock door, turn off alarm, relock door
- ❑ Perform another visual check inside
- ❑ Turn on lights
- ❑ Open safe, remove cash register tills
- ❑ Count money (in office)
- ❑ Turn on computers
- ❑ Turn on air or heat
- ❑ Start daily task list
- ❑ Prepare lunch and break schedules
- ❑ Activate displays, turn on televisions/radios
- ❑ Place/take down display signs as needed
- ❑ Check e-mail and respond if necessary
- ❑ _____
- ❑ _____

Closing Checklist

Date _____

- ☐ After all customers have left, lock door(s)
- ☐ Bring any product from outside into the store
- ☐ Extinguish exterior and front lights
- ☐ Place "closed" sign
- ☐ Close out registers
- ☐ Clean and restock restrooms
- ☐ Return all non-defective merchandise to shelves
- ☐ Move defective merchandise to back room
- ☐ Dust and mop, empty trash
- ☐ Count registers and balance
- ☐ Settle all credit card machines
- ☐ Generate detailed batch listing
- ☐ Transmit batch
- ☐ Place all tills in safe and lock
- ☐ Turn off all electronic equipment
- ☐ Set the alarm, exit and lock doors
- ☐ _____
- ☐ _____

Opening Checklist

Date _____

- ☐ Arrive 15-30 minutes prior to opening
- ☐ Perform a visual check, if concerned call 911
- ☐ Never open the store alone, always have at least one other coworker present
- ☐ Unlock door, turn off alarm, relock door
- ☐ Perform another visual check inside
- ☐ Turn on lights
- ☐ Open safe, remove cash register tills
- ☐ Count money (in office)
- ☐ Turn on computers
- ☐ Turn on air or heat
- ☐ Start daily task list
- ☐ Prepare lunch and break schedules
- ☐ Activate displays, turn on televisions/radios
- ☐ Place/take down display signs as needed
- ☐ Check e-mail and respond if necessary
- ☐ _____
- ☐ _____

Closing Checklist

Date _____

- ❑ After all customers have left, lock door(s)
- ❑ Bring any product from outside into the store
- ❑ Extinguish exterior and front lights
- ❑ Place "closed" sign
- ❑ Close out registers
- ❑ Clean and restock restrooms
- ❑ Return all non-defective merchandise to shelves
- ❑ Move defective merchandise to back room
- ❑ Dust and mop, empty trash
- ❑ Count registers and balance
- ❑ Settle all credit card machines
- ❑ Generate detailed batch listing
- ❑ Transmit batch
- ❑ Place all tills in safe and lock
- ❑ Turn off all electronic equipment
- ❑ Set the alarm, exit and lock doors
- ❑ _____
- ❑ _____

Opening Checklist

Date _____

- ❑ Arrive 15-30 minutes prior to opening
- ❑ Perform a visual check, if concerned call 911
- ❑ Never open the store alone, always have at least one other coworker present
- ❑ Unlock door, turn off alarm, relock door
- ❑ Perform another visual check inside
- ❑ Turn on lights
- ❑ Open safe, remove cash register tills
- ❑ Count money (in office)
- ❑ Turn on computers
- ❑ Turn on air or heat
- ❑ Start daily task list
- ❑ Prepare lunch and break schedules
- ❑ Activate displays, turn on televisions/radios
- ❑ Place/take down display signs as needed
- ❑ Check e-mail and respond if necessary
- ❑ _____
- ❑ _____

Closing Checklist

Date _____

- ☐ After all customers have left, lock door(s)
- ☐ Bring any product from outside into the store
- ☐ Extinguish exterior and front lights
- ☐ Place "closed" sign
- ☐ Close out registers
- ☐ Clean and restock restrooms
- ☐ Return all non-defective merchandise to shelves
- ☐ Move defective merchandise to back room
- ☐ Dust and mop, empty trash
- ☐ Count registers and balance
- ☐ Settle all credit card machines
- ☐ Generate detailed batch listing
- ☐ Transmit batch
- ☐ Place all tills in safe and lock
- ☐ Turn off all electronic equipment
- ☐ Set the alarm, exit and lock doors
- ☐ _____
- ☐ _____

Opening Checklist

Date _____

- ☐ Arrive 15-30 minutes prior to opening
- ☐ Perform a visual check, if concerned call 911
- ☐ Never open the store alone, always have at least one other coworker present
- ☐ Unlock door, turn off alarm, relock door
- ☐ Perform another visual check inside
- ☐ Turn on lights
- ☐ Open safe, remove cash register tills
- ☐ Count money (in office)
- ☐ Turn on computers
- ☐ Turn on air or heat
- ☐ Start daily task list
- ☐ Prepare lunch and break schedules
- ☐ Activate displays, turn on televisions/radios
- ☐ Place/take down display signs as needed
- ☐ Check e-mail and respond if necessary
- ☐ _____
- ☐ _____

Closing Checklist

Date _____

- ☐ After all customers have left, lock door(s)
- ☐ Bring any product from outside into the store
- ☐ Extinguish exterior and front lights
- ☐ Place "closed" sign
- ☐ Close out registers
- ☐ Clean and restock restrooms
- ☐ Return all non-defective merchandise to shelves
- ☐ Move defective merchandise to back room
- ☐ Dust and mop, empty trash
- ☐ Count registers and balance
- ☐ Settle all credit card machines
- ☐ Generate detailed batch listing
- ☐ Transmit batch
- ☐ Place all tills in safe and lock
- ☐ Turn off all electronic equipment
- ☐ Set the alarm, exit and lock doors
- ☐ _____
- ☐ _____

Opening Checklist

Date _____

- ☐ Arrive 15-30 minutes prior to opening
- ☐ Perform a visual check, if concerned call 911
- ☐ Never open the store alone, always have at least one other coworker present
- ☐ Unlock door, turn off alarm, relock door
- ☐ Perform another visual check inside
- ☐ Turn on lights
- ☐ Open safe, remove cash register tills
- ☐ Count money (in office)
- ☐ Turn on computers
- ☐ Turn on air or heat
- ☐ Start daily task list
- ☐ Prepare lunch and break schedules
- ☐ Activate displays, turn on televisions/radios
- ☐ Place/take down display signs as needed
- ☐ Check e-mail and respond if necessary
- ☐ _____
- ☐ _____

Closing Checklist

Date _____

- ☐ After all customers have left, lock door(s)
- ☐ Bring any product from outside into the store
- ☐ Extinguish exterior and front lights
- ☐ Place "closed" sign
- ☐ Close out registers
- ☐ Clean and restock restrooms
- ☐ Return all non-defective merchandise to shelves
- ☐ Move defective merchandise to back room
- ☐ Dust and mop, empty trash
- ☐ Count registers and balance
- ☐ Settle all credit card machines
- ☐ Generate detailed batch listing
- ☐ Transmit batch
- ☐ Place all tills in safe and lock
- ☐ Turn off all electronic equipment
- ☐ Set the alarm, exit and lock doors
- ☐ _____
- ☐ _____

Opening Checklist

Date _____

- ❑ Arrive 15-30 minutes prior to opening
- ❑ Perform a visual check, if concerned call 911
- ❑ Never open the store alone, always have at least one other coworker present
- ❑ Unlock door, turn off alarm, relock door
- ❑ Perform another visual check inside
- ❑ Turn on lights
- ❑ Open safe, remove cash register tills
- ❑ Count money (in office)
- ❑ Turn on computers
- ❑ Turn on air or heat
- ❑ Start daily task list
- ❑ Prepare lunch and break schedules
- ❑ Activate displays, turn on televisions/radios
- ❑ Place/take down display signs as needed
- ❑ Check e-mail and respond if necessary
- ❑ _____
- ❑ _____

Closing Checklist

Date _____

- ☐ After all customers have left, lock door(s)
- ☐ Bring any product from outside into the store
- ☐ Extinguish exterior and front lights
- ☐ Place "closed" sign
- ☐ Close out registers
- ☐ Clean and restock restrooms
- ☐ Return all non-defective merchandise to shelves
- ☐ Move defective merchandise to back room
- ☐ Dust and mop, empty trash
- ☐ Count registers and balance
- ☐ Settle all credit card machines
- ☐ Generate detailed batch listing
- ☐ Transmit batch
- ☐ Place all tills in safe and lock
- ☐ Turn off all electronic equipment
- ☐ Set the alarm, exit and lock doors
- ☐ _____
- ☐ _____

Opening Checklist

Date _____

- ☐ Arrive 15-30 minutes prior to opening
- ☐ Perform a visual check, if concerned call 911
- ☐ Never open the store alone, always have at least one other coworker present
- ☐ Unlock door, turn off alarm, relock door
- ☐ Perform another visual check inside
- ☐ Turn on lights
- ☐ Open safe, remove cash register tills
- ☐ Count money (in office)
- ☐ Turn on computers
- ☐ Turn on air or heat
- ☐ Start daily task list
- ☐ Prepare lunch and break schedules
- ☐ Activate displays, turn on televisions/radios
- ☐ Place/take down display signs as needed
- ☐ Check e-mail and respond if necessary
- ☐ _____
- ☐ _____

Closing Checklist

Date _____

- ☐ After all customers have left, lock door(s)
- ☐ Bring any product from outside into the store
- ☐ Extinguish exterior and front lights
- ☐ Place "closed" sign
- ☐ Close out registers
- ☐ Clean and restock restrooms
- ☐ Return all non-defective merchandise to shelves
- ☐ Move defective merchandise to back room
- ☐ Dust and mop, empty trash
- ☐ Count registers and balance
- ☐ Settle all credit card machines
- ☐ Generate detailed batch listing
- ☐ Transmit batch
- ☐ Place all tills in safe and lock
- ☐ Turn off all electronic equipment
- ☐ Set the alarm, exit and lock doors
- ☐ _____
- ☐ _____

Opening Checklist

Date _____

- ☐ Arrive 15-30 minutes prior to opening
- ☐ Perform a visual check, if concerned call 911
- ☐ Never open the store alone, always have at least one other coworker present
- ☐ Unlock door, turn off alarm, relock door
- ☐ Perform another visual check inside
- ☐ Turn on lights
- ☐ Open safe, remove cash register tills
- ☐ Count money (in office)
- ☐ Turn on computers
- ☐ Turn on air or heat
- ☐ Start daily task list
- ☐ Prepare lunch and break schedules
- ☐ Activate displays, turn on televisions/radios
- ☐ Place/take down display signs as needed
- ☐ Check e-mail and respond if necessary
- ☐ _____
- ☐ _____

Closing Checklist

Date _____

- ☐ After all customers have left, lock door(s)
- ☐ Bring any product from outside into the store
- ☐ Extinguish exterior and front lights
- ☐ Place "closed" sign
- ☐ Close out registers
- ☐ Clean and restock restrooms
- ☐ Return all non-defective merchandise to shelves
- ☐ Move defective merchandise to back room
- ☐ Dust and mop, empty trash
- ☐ Count registers and balance
- ☐ Settle all credit card machines
- ☐ Generate detailed batch listing
- ☐ Transmit batch
- ☐ Place all tills in safe and lock
- ☐ Turn off all electronic equipment
- ☐ Set the alarm, exit and lock doors
- ☐ _____
- ☐ _____

Opening Checklist

Date _____

- ☐ Arrive 15-30 minutes prior to opening
- ☐ Perform a visual check, if concerned call 911
- ☐ Never open the store alone, always have at least one other coworker present
- ☐ Unlock door, turn off alarm, relock door
- ☐ Perform another visual check inside
- ☐ Turn on lights
- ☐ Open safe, remove cash register tills
- ☐ Count money (in office)
- ☐ Turn on computers
- ☐ Turn on air or heat
- ☐ Start daily task list
- ☐ Prepare lunch and break schedules
- ☐ Activate displays, turn on televisions/radios
- ☐ Place/take down display signs as needed
- ☐ Check e-mail and respond if necessary
- ☐ _____
- ☐ _____

Closing Checklist

Date _____

- ☐ After all customers have left, lock door(s)
- ☐ Bring any product from outside into the store
- ☐ Extinguish exterior and front lights
- ☐ Place "closed" sign
- ☐ Close out registers
- ☐ Clean and restock restrooms
- ☐ Return all non-defective merchandise to shelves
- ☐ Move defective merchandise to back room
- ☐ Dust and mop, empty trash
- ☐ Count registers and balance
- ☐ Settle all credit card machines
- ☐ Generate detailed batch listing
- ☐ Transmit batch
- ☐ Place all tills in safe and lock
- ☐ Turn off all electronic equipment
- ☐ Set the alarm, exit and lock doors
- ☐ _____
- ☐ _____

Opening Checklist

Date _____

- ☐ Arrive 15-30 minutes prior to opening
- ☐ Perform a visual check, if concerned call 911
- ☐ Never open the store alone, always have at least one other coworker present
- ☐ Unlock door, turn off alarm, relock door
- ☐ Perform another visual check inside
- ☐ Turn on lights
- ☐ Open safe, remove cash register tills
- ☐ Count money (in office)
- ☐ Turn on computers
- ☐ Turn on air or heat
- ☐ Start daily task list
- ☐ Prepare lunch and break schedules
- ☐ Activate displays, turn on televisions/radios
- ☐ Place/take down display signs as needed
- ☐ Check e-mail and respond if necessary
- ☐ _____
- ☐ _____

Closing Checklist

Date _____

- ☐ After all customers have left, lock door(s)
- ☐ Bring any product from outside into the store
- ☐ Extinguish exterior and front lights
- ☐ Place "closed" sign
- ☐ Close out registers
- ☐ Clean and restock restrooms
- ☐ Return all non-defective merchandise to shelves
- ☐ Move defective merchandise to back room
- ☐ Dust and mop, empty trash
- ☐ Count registers and balance
- ☐ Settle all credit card machines
- ☐ Generate detailed batch listing
- ☐ Transmit batch
- ☐ Place all tills in safe and lock
- ☐ Turn off all electronic equipment
- ☐ Set the alarm, exit and lock doors
- ☐ _____
- ☐ _____

Opening Checklist

Date _____

- ❑ Arrive 15-30 minutes prior to opening
- ❑ Perform a visual check, if concerned call 911
- ❑ Never open the store alone, always have at least one other coworker present
- ❑ Unlock door, turn off alarm, relock door
- ❑ Perform another visual check inside
- ❑ Turn on lights
- ❑ Open safe, remove cash register tills
- ❑ Count money (in office)
- ❑ Turn on computers
- ❑ Turn on air or heat
- ❑ Start daily task list
- ❑ Prepare lunch and break schedules
- ❑ Activate displays, turn on televisions/radios
- ❑ Place/take down display signs as needed
- ❑ Check e-mail and respond if necessary
- ❑ _____
- ❑ _____

Closing Checklist

Date _____

- ❑ After all customers have left, lock door(s)
- ❑ Bring any product from outside into the store
- ❑ Extinguish exterior and front lights
- ❑ Place "closed" sign
- ❑ Close out registers
- ❑ Clean and restock restrooms
- ❑ Return all non-defective merchandise to shelves
- ❑ Move defective merchandise to back room
- ❑ Dust and mop, empty trash
- ❑ Count registers and balance
- ❑ Settle all credit card machines
- ❑ Generate detailed batch listing
- ❑ Transmit batch
- ❑ Place all tills in safe and lock
- ❑ Turn off all electronic equipment
- ❑ Set the alarm, exit and lock doors
- ❑ _____
- ❑ _____

Opening Checklist

Date _____

- ❏ Arrive 15-30 minutes prior to opening
- ❏ Perform a visual check, if concerned call 911
- ❏ Never open the store alone, always have at least one other coworker present
- ❏ Unlock door, turn off alarm, relock door
- ❏ Perform another visual check inside
- ❏ Turn on lights
- ❏ Open safe, remove cash register tills
- ❏ Count money (in office)
- ❏ Turn on computers
- ❏ Turn on air or heat
- ❏ Start daily task list
- ❏ Prepare lunch and break schedules
- ❏ Activate displays, turn on televisions/radios
- ❏ Place/take down display signs as needed
- ❏ Check e-mail and respond if necessary
- ❏ _____
- ❏ _____

Closing Checklist

Date _____

- ☐ After all customers have left, lock door(s)
- ☐ Bring any product from outside into the store
- ☐ Extinguish exterior and front lights
- ☐ Place "closed" sign
- ☐ Close out registers
- ☐ Clean and restock restrooms
- ☐ Return all non-defective merchandise to shelves
- ☐ Move defective merchandise to back room
- ☐ Dust and mop, empty trash
- ☐ Count registers and balance
- ☐ Settle all credit card machines
- ☐ Generate detailed batch listing
- ☐ Transmit batch
- ☐ Place all tills in safe and lock
- ☐ Turn off all electronic equipment
- ☐ Set the alarm, exit and lock doors
- ☐ _____
- ☐ _____

Opening Checklist

Date _____

- ☐ Arrive 15-30 minutes prior to opening
- ☐ Perform a visual check, if concerned call 911
- ☐ Never open the store alone, always have at least one other coworker present
- ☐ Unlock door, turn off alarm, relock door
- ☐ Perform another visual check inside
- ☐ Turn on lights
- ☐ Open safe, remove cash register tills
- ☐ Count money (in office)
- ☐ Turn on computers
- ☐ Turn on air or heat
- ☐ Start daily task list
- ☐ Prepare lunch and break schedules
- ☐ Activate displays, turn on televisions/radios
- ☐ Place/take down display signs as needed
- ☐ Check e-mail and respond if necessary
- ☐ _____
- ☐ _____

Closing Checklist

Date _____

- ☐ After all customers have left, lock door(s)
- ☐ Bring any product from outside into the store
- ☐ Extinguish exterior and front lights
- ☐ Place "closed" sign
- ☐ Close out registers
- ☐ Clean and restock restrooms
- ☐ Return all non-defective merchandise to shelves
- ☐ Move defective merchandise to back room
- ☐ Dust and mop, empty trash
- ☐ Count registers and balance
- ☐ Settle all credit card machines
- ☐ Generate detailed batch listing
- ☐ Transmit batch
- ☐ Place all tills in safe and lock
- ☐ Turn off all electronic equipment
- ☐ Set the alarm, exit and lock doors
- ☐ _____
- ☐ _____

Opening Checklist

Date _____

- ☐ Arrive 15-30 minutes prior to opening
- ☐ Perform a visual check, if concerned call 911
- ☐ Never open the store alone, always have at least one other coworker present
- ☐ Unlock door, turn off alarm, relock door
- ☐ Perform another visual check inside
- ☐ Turn on lights
- ☐ Open safe, remove cash register tills
- ☐ Count money (in office)
- ☐ Turn on computers
- ☐ Turn on air or heat
- ☐ Start daily task list
- ☐ Prepare lunch and break schedules
- ☐ Activate displays, turn on televisions/radios
- ☐ Place/take down display signs as needed
- ☐ Check e-mail and respond if necessary
- ☐ _____
- ☐ _____

Closing Checklist

Date _____

- ☐ After all customers have left, lock door(s)
- ☐ Bring any product from outside into the store
- ☐ Extinguish exterior and front lights
- ☐ Place "closed" sign
- ☐ Close out registers
- ☐ Clean and restock restrooms
- ☐ Return all non-defective merchandise to shelves
- ☐ Move defective merchandise to back room
- ☐ Dust and mop, empty trash
- ☐ Count registers and balance
- ☐ Settle all credit card machines
- ☐ Generate detailed batch listing
- ☐ Transmit batch
- ☐ Place all tills in safe and lock
- ☐ Turn off all electronic equipment
- ☐ Set the alarm, exit and lock doors
- ☐ _____
- ☐ _____

Opening Checklist

Date _____

- ❏ Arrive 15-30 minutes prior to opening
- ❏ Perform a visual check, if concerned call 911
- ❏ Never open the store alone, always have at least one other coworker present
- ❏ Unlock door, turn off alarm, relock door
- ❏ Perform another visual check inside
- ❏ Turn on lights
- ❏ Open safe, remove cash register tills
- ❏ Count money (in office)
- ❏ Turn on computers
- ❏ Turn on air or heat
- ❏ Start daily task list
- ❏ Prepare lunch and break schedules
- ❏ Activate displays, turn on televisions/radios
- ❏ Place/take down display signs as needed
- ❏ Check e-mail and respond if necessary
- ❏ _____
- ❏ _____

Closing Checklist

Date _____

- ☐ After all customers have left, lock door(s)
- ☐ Bring any product from outside into the store
- ☐ Extinguish exterior and front lights
- ☐ Place "closed" sign
- ☐ Close out registers
- ☐ Clean and restock restrooms
- ☐ Return all non-defective merchandise to shelves
- ☐ Move defective merchandise to back room
- ☐ Dust and mop, empty trash
- ☐ Count registers and balance
- ☐ Settle all credit card machines
- ☐ Generate detailed batch listing
- ☐ Transmit batch
- ☐ Place all tills in safe and lock
- ☐ Turn off all electronic equipment
- ☐ Set the alarm, exit and lock doors
- ☐ _____
- ☐ _____

Thank you for purchasing this journal. We hope you enjoy blogging as much as we do!

Look for our other books on Amazon!

www.ingramcontent.com/pod-product-compliance
Lightning Source LLC
Chambersburg PA
CBHW070423190526
45169CB00003B/1391